Activities to Accompany
PsychNow 2e

Charyl R. Glover

THOMSON LEARNING

CUSTOM PUBLISHING

COPYRIGHT © 2000 by Thomson Learning

Printed in the United States of America

For more information, contact Thomson Learning Custom Publishing, 5101 Madison Road, Cincinnati, OH 45227, or electronically at http://www.itpcustomsolutions.com

Thomson Learning Publishing Europe
Berkshire House 168-173
High Holborn
London, WC1V 7AA, England

Thomas Nelson Australia
102 Dodds Street
South Melbourne 3205
Victoria, Australia

Nelson Canada
1120 Birchmount Road
Scarborough, Ontario
Canada M1K 5G4

Thomson Learning Publishing GmbH
Königswinterer Strasse 418
53227 Bonn, Germany

Thomson Learning Editores
Campos Eliseos 385, Piso 7
Col. Polanco
11560 México D.F. México

Thomson Learning Publishing Asia
221 Henderson Road
#05-10 Henderson Building
Singapore 0315

Thomson Learning Publishing Japan
Hirakawacho Kyowa Building, 3F
2-2-1 Hirakawacho
Chiyoda-ku, Tokyo 102, Japan

Thomson Learning Publishing Southern Africa
Building 18, Constantia Park
240 Old Pretoria Road
Halfway House, 1685 South Africa

All rights reserved. No part of this work covered by the copyright hereon may be reproduced or used in any form or by any means—graphic, electronic, or mechanical, including photocopying, recording, taping, or information storage and retrieval systems—without the written permission of the publisher.

ISBN 0-324-06617-1

These exercises are meant to accompany the PsychNow! CD-ROM. It is assumed that students will complete all activities in the Explore sections, in the Lesson sections, and in the Apply sections prior to completing the exercises.

--Charyl R. Glover

Name:_____.

Course and section number: _____.

MODULE 1A: STUDY SKILLS
If you need extra space- attach another piece of paper

1. Identify the type of learner that you are and why you think you are that type of learner.

2. What can you do as a student to adjust your study skills to match your learning style?

3. From the Lesson section, pick the areas that you personally feel that you need to improve. How can you improve those skills for this class? Be specific.

Name:_____.

Course and section number: _____.

MODULE 1B: PSYCHOLOGY & IT'S HISTORY
If you need extra space- Attach another piece of paper

1. After completing the Lesson section, are there any areas that you feel have been left out of Psychology? In other words, does the history of Psychology seem incomplete?

2. After completing the Lesson section, were you surprised by any areas of Psychology- was there something that you didn't originally consider to be part of Psychology?

3. What societal issues (for example, think of issues that are important to parents, workers, adolescents, etc.) do you think should be addressed or need to be addressed in the next 10 years by Psychology?

Name:_____.

Course and section number: _____.

MODULE 1C: RESEARCH METHODS
If you need extra space- attach another piece of paper

1. After completing the Explore and Lesson sections, in what ways did Dr. Amabile have control over the variables? Identify all.

2. How is the independent variable related to the experimental group?

3. Can a correlation study have an independent variable? Can it have a dependent variable?

4. In terms of evidence collected, why would a researcher want to conduct a "true experiment" rather than a correlation?

5. Thinking about your answer to question #4, why are correlation studies conducted at all?

Name:_____.

Course and section number: _____.

MODULE 1C: RESEARCH METHODS
If you need extra space- attach another piece of paper

6. Identify a "true experiment" OR a correlation study from a source other than your book or the CD (for example- a newspaper article, a journal article, a news report, the internet). The study should be related to Psychology in some way.

       Briefly describe the Study.

       What type of experiment is it (true experiment or correlation)?

       What is the hypothesis?

       Was there a control group? What was it?

       Was there an experimental group? What was it?

       Identify the independent and dependent variables.

Name:_____.

Course and section number: _____.

MODULE 1D: CRITICAL THINKING IN PSYCHOLOGY
If you need extra space- Attach another piece of paper

1. Answer the question from the Explore section again, this time using the 5 critical thinking skills outlined in the Lesson section.

2. Identify a statement concerning human behavior that you heard on a television or radio news program, or that you read on the internet or in a news article. The statement needs to either: (1) make some prediction about human behavior or (2) explain some aspect of human behavior. Practice on the Apply section first.

    What was the statement?

    Evaluate that statement based on:

        What was the source?

        Was the statement based on evidence?

        Was the evidence anecdotal?

        Was the evidence based on a true experiment or a correlation?

        Was causation implied?

        Are there alternate explanations?

Name:_____.

Course and section number: _____.

MODULE 2A: Neurons and Synaptic Connections
If you need extra space- attach another piece of paper

After completing the Lesson section:

1. What material is the brain composed of?

2. Approximately how many other neurons can 1 neuron connect to?

3. What is the importance of having neurons communicate with other neurons?

4. What would happen if some of these connections were cut?

5. What is the importance of the myelin sheath?

6. What happens if the neurotransmitters are not released into the synaptic gap?

7. What happens if the receptor sites are blocked from receiving the neurotransmitter substance?

Name:_____.

Course and section number: _____.

MODULE 2B: BRAIN & BEHAVIOR
If you need extra space- Attach another piece of paper

1. In the Lesson section, click on the motor region of the frontal lobe and the somatosensory area of the parietal lobe. What is the relationship between the size of the brain area and the size of the corresponding body part?

2. Based on what you read in the Lesson section about the cerebral cortex and cerebrum in humans and in other species, why is it so much larger in humans?

3. Consider the relationship between the percentage of neural connections that exist in the cerebrum compared to other areas of the brain. What does this tell us about the function of the cerebrum? Why are there so many neural connections?

4. Take 1 activity you personally do and describe **all** areas of the brain involved and how each area is involved in the activity.

Name:_____.

Course and section number: _____.

MODULE 2C: SLEEP & DREAMING
If you need extra space- attach another piece of paper

1. After revealing all of the facts in the Explore section, why is sleep so important?

2. From the Lesson section, identify what happens to neural transmissions during each stage of sleep (please note that brain wave activity indicates neural activity).

3. Why might there be an increase in neural activity during REM sleep, similar to when someone is awake?

4. In the Apply section make each false statement true.

Name:_____.

Course and section number: _____.

MODULE 2D: PSYCHOACTIVE DRUGS
If you need extra space- Attach another piece of paper

1. How might stimulants affect the transmission of neurotransmitters? For a hint- look at the Lesson section: What are the effects of the stimulants and what is their purpose?

2. How might depressants affect the transmission of neurotransmitters: What are the effects of the depressants and what is their purpose?

3. Look at the continuum of drugs in the Lesson section. Why are some drugs like Mescaline, LSD, and Psilocybin at the extreme end of the stimulant scale and drugs like Nicotine, Caffeine, and Cocaine near the more neutral end of the stimulant scale? Similarly, why are drugs like Morphine, Barbiturates, and Heroin at the extreme end of the depressant scale and drugs like Alcohol and Benzodiazepines closer to the neutral end?

Name:_____.

Course and section number: _____.

MODULE 3A: VISION & HEARING
If you need extra space- Attach another piece of paper

1. After completing the Lesson and Apply sections, in what ways are the transduction processes for vision and hearing similar? You should pay attention to the different structures and their function (note that not all structures and functions will match up).

Name:_____.

Course and section number: _____.

MODULE 3B: CHEMICAL AND SOMESTHETIC SENSES
If you need extra space- Attach another piece of paper

1. Click on chemical and kinesthetic icon and complete the activities in the Explore section:
    A. Why was trial #2 so hard?

    B. Why was trial #3 easier than trial #2? If it wasn't harder for you, can you imagine why it would be harder for most people?

    C. Why was trial #4 slower than trial #1? If trial #4 wasn't slower, can you imagine why it could have been slower?

2. When have you experienced the different types of somatic pain?

3. From your own experiences what are some areas of your body where there are probably more skin receptors? Why would these areas have more skin receptors?

4. After completing 3A and 3B, what is the relationship between the complexity of transduction and the particular sense? Do some senses have more complex pathways of transduction than other senses? Which ones? Why?

Name:_____.

Course and section number: _____.

MODULE 3B: CHEMICAL AND SOMESTHETIC SENSES
If you need extra space- Attach another piece of paper

5. After completing all of the sections you should know that different qualities, like red or blue, bitter or sweet, musky or floral trigger different receptors that send different signals to the brain. But, how does our brain know if the object is more blue (or a brighter blue) than something else, sweeter than something else, or more musky than something else?

6. Think about a normal day of your life. How are each of your 5 senses involved in your daily life activities? Provide examples.

Name:_____.

Course and section number: _____.

MODULE 3C: PERCEPTION
If you need extra space- Attach another piece of paper

1. Draw a picture or find a picture from a magazine that makes use of at least 3 of the monocular depth cues. Identify what the depth cues are and how they have been used to provide depth in that picture. Be sure to provide a copy of the picture.

2. Find an example of how you have used top-down processing in your own life.

Name:_____.

Course and section number: _____.

MODULE 4A: MOTIVATION
If you need extra space- attach another piece of paper

1. In the Lesson section, relate your college experience to Mortimer's quest:

    A. Do you have a need you are trying to reduce?

    B. Assess your college experience using arousal theory.

    C. What "pushes" and "pulls" are there on your educational goal?

    D. For you, is a college degree high or low in incentive value?

    E. Have you experienced a "fork in the road" along your educational path? If so, which path did you take?

    F. What types of needs are you meeting with a college education?

Name:_____.

Course and section number: _____.

MODULE 4B: EMOTION
If you need extra space- attach another piece of paper

1. What cues, other than facial expression can we use to interpret someone's emotions?

2. Is it possible to hide our facial expressions or emotions? Why would people want to hide them?

3. Are facial expressions learned or are they simply biological responses?

Name:_____.

Course and section number: _____.

MODULE 4C: COPING WITH EMOTION
If you need extra space- attach another piece of paper

1. How do you deal with the anxiety you experience in college? Use the list of 10 methods defined in the Explore and Lesson sections. You may use a combination of these methods.

2. Do you tend to use problem-focused coping styles or emotion-focused coping styles?

3. If you already use problem-focused coping styles, go through each of the 5 steps from the Lesson section and show how you apply those steps to a particular problem. If you do not already use problem-focused coping style, use the 5 steps to show how you could use the problem-focused coping style.

Name:_____.

Course and section number: _____.

MODULE 4D: STRESS & HEALTH
If you need extra space- attach another piece of paper

1. In your school work, family life, or at work, describe how each of the 5 factors listed in the Lesson section contribute to your stress level.

2. Has your health ever been affected by stress? If so, how?

3. Take the stress test in the Apply section. How did you score? Did this surprise you?

4. Is there anything you can do to alleviate stress?

Name:_____.

Course and section number: _____.

MODULE 4E: HUMAN SEXUALITY
If you need extra space- attach another piece of paper

1. How sexually well-informed are you based on how well you answered the questions in the Explore section?

2. Why is it important to know the similarities and differences between men and women in terms of sexual response?

3. How are men and women similar and different in terms of their sexual response cycles?

4. Do you have a lot of stereotypes about the opposite sex? If so, what are they?

Name:_____.

Course and section number: _____.

MODULE 5A: CLASSICAL CONDITIONING
If you need extra space- attach another piece of paper

1. After completing the Lesson section, come up with 3 examples of unconditioned stimuli and their unconditioned responses (examples that were not from the CD, the book or that were discussed in class).

2. Using the unconditioned stimuli and unconditioned responses from question #1, create a conditioned stimulus and a conditioned response to go with each one.

3. When does a conditioned response form?

4. Can any stimulus form any **unconditioned** response? Why?

5. What comes first, the CS & CR pair or the UCS & UCR pair?

6. After completing the Apply section, come up with your own example of a time in your life when you experienced classical conditioning. Be sure to identify the unconditioned stimulus, the unconditioned response, the conditioned stimulus, and the conditioned response.

Name:_____.

Course and section number: _____.

MODULE 5B: OPERANT CONDITIONING
If you need extra space- attach another piece of paper

1. After completing the Apply section, come up with your own examples of:

   A. Positive reinforcement:

   B. Negative reinforcement:

   C. Punishment:

   D. Extinction:

Name:_____.

Course and section number: _____.

MODULE 5C: OBSERVATIONAL LEARNING
If you need extra space- attach another piece of paper

1. After completing the Lesson section, how is observational learning different from learning theory?

2. Based on what you read in the Lesson section, would a child who is spanked learn aggressiveness? Why or why not?

3. Based on what you read in the Lesson section, would a child who watches Southpark learn aggressiveness? Why or why not?

Name:_____.

Course and section number: _____.

MODULE 5D: MEMORY SYSTEMS
If you need extra space- attach another piece of paper

1. After completing the Explore section, how could Chris remember that story even though it never happened?

2. Why is sensory memory necessary?

3. In the lesson section, complete the exercises entitled "short-term memory."

    A. How many digits were you able to recall correctly in the lists?

    B. Did you get all of the lists correct? Which did you get wrong?

    C. Did you find it easier to remember the letters? Why or why not?

Name:_____.

Course and section number: _____.

MODULE 5D: MEMORY SYSTEMS
If you need extra space- attach another piece of paper

4. In the Lesson section, complete the exercise entitled "long-term memory."

    A. Come up with your own example of episodic memory.

    B. Come up with your own example of semantic memory.

    C. Come up with your own example of procedural memory.

5. What areas in your life are most susceptible to forgetting? Why?

6. Interference occurs when new information interferes with something previously learned or vice versa (when old information interferes with learning new information). Keeping this in mind and after completing the Apply section, does there seem to be a time limit on when interference can take place? In other words, after a certain amount of time has passed between learning the old information and learning the new information is interference, in either direction, less likely to occur or unable occur?

7. Is there anything you can do to help prevent interference from occurring?

Name:_____.

Course and section number: _____.

MODULE 5F: COGNITION & LANGUAGE
If you need extra space- attach another piece of paper

1. In your own life how have you framed a statement to get someone to do something you wanted them to do (think back to when you were a child or teenager and wanted your parents to do something).

2. Identify a time when someone (a friend, advertisement, or a newscaster) has used the framing effect on you.

Name:_____.

Course and section number: _____.

MODULE 5G: PROBLEM SOLVING AND CREATIVITY
If you need extra space-attach another piece of paper

1. Complete the Explore section and the Lesson section, rate the answers you gave in the Explore section in terms of fluency, flexibility, and originality.

2. Can we measure creativity in an objective way? Why or why not?

3. Using the 5 steps in the Lesson section evaluate how you solved the key link problem in the Explore section. Did you leave any of the 5 steps out? If so, go back and try to solve the problem again using those steps.

4. Is it still "creative" if we follow steps to be creative problem solvers?

Name:_____.

Course and section number: _____.

MODULE 6A: INFANT DEVELOPMENT
If you need extra space- attach another piece of paper

1. How does emotional responsiveness change over the course of the first 15 months of life?

2. Why do you think this change in emotional responsiveness occurs?

3. How are the emotions infants are capable of expressing involved with the bonding process between parent and child?

Name:_____.

Course and section number: _____.

MODULE 6B: CHILD DEVELOPMENT
If you need extra space- attach another piece of paper

1. Complete the Explore section. Discuss how a child's thinking is related to his or her style of play.

2. What expectations do parents or caregivers have for children in the sensorimotor stage of development?

3. What expectations do parents or teachers have for children in the preoperational stage of development?

4. What expectations do parents or teachers have for children in the concrete operational stage of development?

5. What expectations do parents or teachers have for children in the formal operational stage of development?

Name:_____.

Course and section number: _____.

MODULE 6C: ADOLESCENT DEVELOPMENT
If you need extra space- attach another piece of paper

1. Take the quiz in the Apply section. What stage of development are you at according to the quiz? Do you agree, why or why not?

2. In the Explore section it is stated that there are not many formal rites of passage that mark the transition from childhood to adolescence in American culture. Thinking back to this time period in your own life, what informal rites of passage did you experience?

3. Are there any informal rites of passage in America that mark the transition from adolescence to adulthood? What are they?

Name:_____.

Course and section number: _____.

MODULE 6D: ADULT DEVELOPMENT & AGING & DYING
If you need extra space- attach another piece of paper

1. In the Explore section, take the quiz. Which ones did you get wrong? Why did you have that misconception?

2. What are some things that can be done to correct the misconceptions society has about the elderly?

3. Are there things you can do to remain mentally alert in old age?

4. After completing the Lesson section, what are 6 things you can do to have a positive sense of well-being as you age?

5. What do you expect your life to be like when you are 70-years-old?

Name:_____.

Course and section number: _____.

MODULE 7A: THEORIES OF PERSONALITY
If you need extra space- attach another piece of paper

1. In the Explore section, take the self-image test. Was there agreement between who you are and who you want to be?

2. How are the Trait, Psychodynamic, Humanistic, and Behaviorist theories of personality different in terms of how personality is formed?

3. How is self-actualization linked to motivation? (Hint- Module 4A also discussed this)

4. Write down a list of your personality traits and have a friend write down a list of your personality traits (don't peak). Now compare the lists- is there congruency?

Name:_____.

Course and section number: _____.

MODULE 7B: ASSESSMENT
If you need extra space- attach another piece of paper

1. In the Explore section, take the IQ test. What did you think?

2. Is there any way to make a culture-free IQ test?

3. In the Lesson section, assess the 4 methods of assessment. Which do you think is best (take into account predictability, validity, and standardization)?

Name:_____.

Course and section number: _____.

MODULE 7C: ABNORMALITY AND PSYCHOPATHOLOGY
If you need extra space- attach another piece of paper

1. Has anything you ever done been considered abnormal? Why?

2. What criteria do we use to judge normality?

3. Is there any clear-cut definition of abnormal or normal behavior? Explain your answer.

Name:_____.

Course and section number: _____.

MODULE 7D: NON-PSYCHOTIC, PSYCHOTIC AND AFFECTIVE DISORDERS
If you need more space, attach another piece of paper

1. After completing the Lesson section, were you surprised to see some of the disorders included in the list of major psychological disorders? If so, which ones?

2. Discuss how the behavior associated with each disorder in the Lesson section violates a norm.

3. Sometimes we all engage in behavior that may be similar to the behaviors that are characteristic of certain disorders yet we do not really have that disorder. For example, some children are fidgety but do not have Attention Deficit Hyperactivity Disorder, some of us don't like spiders yet do not have a phobia, some people diet but don't have an eating disorder. What is necessary for psychologists to classify certain behaviors as disorders (in other words, when is fidgety behavior not just fidgety behavior but a symptom of ADHD)?

Name:_____.

Course and section number: _____.

MODULE 7E: MAJOR PSYCHOLOGICAL THERAPIES
If you need extra space- attach another piece of paper

1. In the Lesson section, identify the goal of each therapy.

    A. Client-centered

    B. Psychoanalysis

    C. Somatic

    D. Behavior

    E. Cognitive/Behavior

2. In the Lesson section, identify the techniques used in each therapy.

    A. Client-centered

    B. Psychoanalysis

    C. Somatic

    D. Behavior

    E. Cognitive/Behavior

3. How is it possible that the same disorder can be treated in different ways?

Name:_____.

Course and section number: _____.

MODULE 8A: HELPING OTHERS
If you need extra space- attach another piece of paper

1. After reading about Kitty Genovese do you think that could happen now? Why or why not?

2. In the Apply section what are some (mention at least 3 things) things that decrease our likelihood to help other people?

Name:_____.

Course and section number: _____.

MODULE 8B: ATTRIBUTION
If you need extra space- attach another piece of paper

1. In the Explore section, when did you tend to make internal attributions?

2. In the Explore section, when did you tend to make external attributions?

3. Is it easier to change our behavior if we make internal attributions or external attributions?

4. Identify a time when you made the Fundamental Attribution Error.

5. Identify a time when you used the self-serving bias.

6. If adults are capable of thinking logically (look back at Piaget's stage of formal operational thinking) why do we still make the fundamental attribution error and use the self-serving bias?

Name:_____.

Course and section number: _____.

MODULE 8C: SOCIAL INFLUENCE, OBEDIENCE AND CONFORMITY
If you need extra space- attach another piece of paper

1. How long did you continue the activity in the Explore section? Why?

2. Are only teenagers susceptible to peer pressure? Why or why not?

3. Identify some conditions that might make conformity more likely.

4. How do conformity and obedience differ?

Name:_____.

Course and section number: _____.

MODULE 8D: ATTITUDES AND PREJUDICE
If you need extra space- attach another piece of paper

1. In the Lesson 2 section click on the table icon. What results do you think you would find if you administered the survey today?

2. **Check with your instructor before doing this activity. You might need to get permission from your school's internal review board. If so your instructor may opt to skip this assignment.** Give the survey to 10 people to find out their attitudes. In order to do this you will have to make 10 copies of the 23 adjectives listed. Have each person mark whether the adjective describes Americans, Germans, Jews, African Americans, Italians, or Irish. The same adjective can describe more than 1 group. Make sure they do not put their name on the survey. Inform them that their opinions will only be used for a class project- do not tell them it's about stereotypes until after they have completed the survey. What were your results?

3. How is the fundamental attribution error related to stereotypes?

Name:_____.

Course and section number: _____.

MODULE 8D: ATTITUDES AND PREJUDICE
If you need extra space- attach another piece of paper

1. Do your actions always follow your beliefs? Do your actions always follow your emotions? What happens if your actions do not follow your beliefs or your emotions?

2. After completing all of the scenarios in the Apply section, come up with your own Belief statements, Emotion statements, and Action Statements for any issue not already discussed. Some possible issues are: legalization of marijuana, pornography, zero tolerance policies in schools, abortion, or women in the military, or come up with one of your own.

    A. **Scenario:**

Action: 1:

      2:

Emotion: 1:

      2:

Belief: 1:

      2:

Name:_____.

Course and section number: _____.

MODULE 8D : ATTITUDES AND PREJUDICE
If you need extra space- attach another piece of paper

3. What is the link between attitude formation and identity status in adolescence? (see Module 6C for a recap of identity formation)

4. How is prejudice linked to attitude?

Name:_____.

Course and section number: _____.

MODULE 8E: AGGRESSION
If you need extra space- Attach another piece of paper

1. What factors affect whether we label an act as aggressive or non-aggressive?

2. Why are some acts of aggression not clear-cut?

3. After completing the Apply section, what might be helpful in preventing "aggressive" actions?

Name:_____.

Course and section number: _____.

MODULE 8F: ENVIRONMENTAL PSYCHOLOGY
If you need extra space- Attach another piece of paper

1. Do the exercises in the Lesson section. Are the places you study conducive to a "study environment?"

2. Aside from the example given, how is a grocery store set up to encourage you to buy things?

3. Explain the environment of your college or university's student center. Why is it set up that way?

Name:_____.

Course and section number: _____.

MODULE 8G: GENDER & STEREOTYPES
If you need extra space- Attach another piece of paper

1. After completing the Explore section, did you remember more stereotypical terms?

2. Why might people (even if you did not) tend to recall more stereotypical terms? (think back to the structure of memory- Module 5D).

3. What 3 factors reduce the effects of automatic stereotyping?

4. Can you think of a situation when a stereotype you had was wrong?